CW01197174

1 MONTH OF FREE READING

at
www.ForgottenBooks.com

By purchasing this book you are eligible for one month membership to ForgottenBooks.com, giving you unlimited access to our entire collection of over 1,000,000 titles via our web site and mobile apps.

To claim your free month visit: www.forgottenbooks.com/free1222962

* Offer is valid for 45 days from date of purchase. Terms and conditions apply.

ISBN 978-0-428-46766-1
PIBN 11222962

This book is a reproduction of an important historical work. Forgotten Books uses state-of-the-art technology to digitally reconstruct the work, preserving the original format whilst repairing imperfections present in the aged copy. In rare cases, an imperfection in the original, such as a blemish or missing page, may be replicated in our edition. We do, however, repair the vast majority of imperfections successfully; any imperfections that remain are intentionally left to preserve the state of such historical works.

Forgotten Books is a registered trademark of FB &c Ltd.
Copyright © 2018 FB &c Ltd.
FB &c Ltd, Dalton House, 60 Windsor Avenue, London, SW19 2RR.
Company number 08720141. Registered in England and Wales.

For support please visit www.forgottenbooks.com

INDUSTRY AND LABOR PROFILE

Eastern Band of Cherokee Indians

STANDARD TITLE PAGE FOR TECHNICAL REPORTS	1. Report No.	2. Govt. Accession No.	3. Recipient's Catalog No.
4. Title and Subtitle EASTERN BAND OF CHEROKEE INDIANS INDUSTRY AND LABOR PROFILE			5. Report Date September, 1976
			6. Performing Organization Code
7. Author(s) EBCI Planning Board - Bob Blankenship, Larry Callicutt, June Myers			8. Performing Organization Rept. No.
9. Performing Organization Name and Address N.C. DEPT. NATURAL & ECONOMIC RESOURCES DIVISION OF COMMUNITY SERVICES P.O. BOX 27687 - RALEIGH, N.C. 27611			10. Project/Task/Work Unit No.
			11. Contract/Grant No. CPA-NC-04-19-1055
12. Sponsoring Agency Name and Address Department of Housing and Urban Development 451 Seventh Street, S.W. Washington, D.C. 20410			13. Type of Report & Period Covered
			14. Sponsoring Agency Code
15. Supplementary Notes			
16. Abstracts The purpose of this report is to present the facts concerning the industry, labor market and selected community information related to industrial development on the Reservation of the Eastern Band of Cherokee Indians. A detailed supplement of facts for "Industrial Site No. 2 (with building) Available" is included.			
17. Key Words and Document Analysis. (a). Descriptors			
17b. Identifiers/Open-Ended Terms			
17c. COSATI Field/Group			
18. Distribution Statement		19. Security Class (This Report) UNCLASSIFIED	21. No. of Pages
		20. Security Class. (This Page) UNCLASSIFIED	22. Price

Form CFSTI-35 (4-70)

EASTERN BAND OF CHEROKEE INDIANS
INDUSTRY AND LABOR PROFILE

PREPARED FOR:

Eastern Band of Cherokee Indians
John A. Crowe, Principal Chief
Alvin Smith, Vice Chief
Jerome Parker, Advisor

Tribal Council
Jonathan L. Taylor, Chairman
Dan McCoy, Vice Chairman
Joe Bradley
Gerard Parker
Newman Arneach
Bertha Saunooke
Roy Blankenship
John Standingdeer
Wilbur Sequoyah
Thomas Lambert
Bailey Coleman
Gilliam Jackson

PREPARED BY:

Cherokee Planning Board
Dan McCoy, Chairman
Bertha Saunooke, Vice Chairman
Jonathan L. Taylor
June Maldanado
Frell Owl
John A. Crowe
Jim Cooper
Arnold Wachacha
Thomas Lambert

Planning Staff
Bob Blankenship, Tribal Planner
Larry Callicutt, Human Resource
  Specialist
Patricia Smith, Secretary
Margaret French, Assistant Secretary

Aid to Tribal Government
Patricia Dennis, Director
Mark Reed
Wenonah Digh
Jennifer Jackson
Kay Jones
Pat Panther

TECHNICAL ASSISTANCE
PROVIDED BY:

STATE OF NORTH CAROLINA DEPARTMENT
OF NATURAL AND ECONOMIC RESOURCES
  George W. Little, Secretary

Division of Community Assistance
  Robert S. Ewing, Director

Local Planning and Management
Services Section
  Billy Ray Hall, Chief

Western Field Office, Asheville, N.C.
  Alan Lang, Chief Planner
  *June Myers, Planner-in-Charge
  Hermon Rector, Draftsman
  Phyllis Hipps, Stenographer
  Kay Dotson, Stenographer

* Responsible for project.

Preparation of this document was financed in part through an urban grant from the Department of Housing and Urban Development under the provision of Section 701 of the Housing Act of 1954, as amended.

TABLE OF CONTENTS

PART		PAGE
1	OVERVIEW	1
	Land	1
	Sovereignty	2
	Geography	2
	Climate	2
	Population	2
	Government	2
	Administration	3
	Health	4
	Education	4
	Bureau of Indian Affairs	5
	Income	5
	Economy	5
	Culture	5
2	REPORT ON ACTIVE JOB APPLICANTS REGISTERED FOR WORK WITH THE EMPLOYMENT SECURITY OFFICES AND RESIDING IN THE AREA OF CHEROKEE	7
	I. Recruiting Area	7
	II. Population of the Area	7
	III. Workers Residing In the Area Available for Jobs	7
	IV. Types of Potential Workers In the Area Included in the Report	7
	V. Number Of High School Graduates In This Area Which Enter the Labor Force Each Year	7
	VI. Map - Area In Which Active Job Applicants Reside	7
	VII. Active Job Applicants Registered For Work With The Employment Security Commission Office	8
3	INDUSTRIAL DEVELOPMENT FACTS (EDA INDIAN DESK INDUSTRIAL DEVELOPMENT PROGRAM)	13
	I. Date Form Completed	13
	II. Population	13
	III. Labor Market Analysis	13
	IV. Beginning Wage Rates - Prevailing Rates	13
	V. Current Employers (Major Firms)	13
	VI. Transportation	14
	VII. Utilities	14
4	REGULATIONS AND SCHEDULES - CHEROKEE WATER AND SEWER TRIBAL ENTERPRISE	15
	I. Rate Schedules	15
	II. Water Connection Schedule	15
	III. Sewage Connection Charges	16
	IV. Sewer Service Restrictions	16
	V. Monthly Statements	17
	VI. Use Of Water	17
	VII. Continuity and Guarantee Of Service	17

TABLE OF CONTENTS (CONTINUED)

PART			PAGE
	VIII.	Service Connection Limitations	17
	IX.	Maintenance and Repair of Water and Sewage Service Lines	18
	X.	Measurement of Water and Sewage	18
	XI.	General	18
5		COMMUNITY DATA	21
	I.	Civic Data	21
	II.	Accommodations	21
	III.	Education Facilities	21
	IV.	Public Services	21
	V.	Financial Institutions	22
	VI.	Taxes	22
	VII.	Resources	22
6		LABOR MARKET SURVEY AND ANALYSIS	29
	I.	Labor Market Surveys	29
	II.	Labor Market Analysis	35
7		INDUSTRIAL LOCATION FACTORS	37
	I.	General Information	37
	II.	Market Information	37
	III.	Transportation Information	38
	IV.	Industry Characteristics	41
	V.	Resource Availability In Commercial Quantity In Geographic Entity and Contiguous Areas	42
	VI.	Industrial Parks and Sites Serving Growth Community	44
	VII.	Utility Availability In Growth Community	44
	VIII.	Human Resources In Labor Area	45
	IX.	Community Services and Assistance	47
	X.	Public and Private Local Development Organizations	47

MAPS

NUMBER		PAGE
1	AREA IN WHICH ACTIVE JOB APPLICANTS RESIDE	11
2	LAND DEVELOPMENT PLAN - BUILT UP AREA EAST AND WEST SIDES OF THE OCONALUFTEE RIVER	23
3	LAND DEVELOPMENT PLAN - BUILT UP AREA SOCO VALLEY - WEST	25
4	LAND DEVELOPMENT PLAN - BUILT UP AREA SOCO VALLEY - EAST	27
5	DISTANCE TO PRINCIPAL EASTERN CITIES FROM CHEROKEE, NORTH CAROLINA	40

TABLES

1	LABOR SURVEY, LAST WEEK OF FEBRUARY, 1976	30
2	LABOR SURVEY, FIRST WEEK OF JULY, 1976	31
3	LABOR SURVEY, BUSINESSES AND INDUSTRIES OPEN-CLOSED FEBRUARY, 1976	32
4	LABOR SURVEY, 1976 - EMPLOYED, UNEMPLOYED, PART-TIME AND PAYROLL	33
5	LABOR SURVEY - INDIAN POPULATION ONLY, APRIL, 1976 BUREAU OF INDIAN AFFAIRS	34

PART 1

THE EASTERN BAND OF CHEROKEE INDIANS

OVERVIEW

The Cherokees were once a mighty and powerful nation. At the time when the Cherokees came into first contact with the white man (DeSoto in 1540), they claimed 135,000 square miles of territory covering parts of eight states; North Carolina, South Carolina, Georgia, Alabama, Tennessee, Kentucky, Virginia and West Virginia. By the end of the Revolution the Cherokees had lost about half of their land. Between 1785 and 1835 the Cherokee lands had shrunk to a few million acres. By the treaty of New Echota in 1835, all lands east of the Mississippi were ceded to the Federal government. (Of the 40 treaties executed with the Cherokees, the Federal government chose to break each and every one.) Under Article 12 of this Treaty, as amended, provided that such Cherokees as were adverse to removal could become citizens and remain in the State of North Carolina (about 1,200).

The status of those who remained in the State was anomalous. Their connection with the main of the Cherokee Tribe which had been removed to lands west of the Mississippi were severed. They became subject to laws of the State of North Carolina while not admitted to the rights of citizenship. Any interest in the lands formerly held by the Tribe in North Carolina had become divested by the Treaty and even their rights to self-government had ended. North Carolina later granted a charter to the Cherokees authorizing them to exercise limited powers of self-government.

Pressure to force removal of this remnant of Cherokees continued. Funds due them were withheld by the United States Government unless they would remove to the Indian Territory or, would secure an act of the Legislature of North Carolina permitting them to remain permanently within the State. A statute was passed in 1866 granting this permission.

By the purchases of an agent, the Eastern Band of Cherokee Indians had acquired the right to possession of a tract of land in North Carolina, and by the North Carolina Statute of 1866, they had acquired, with the approval of the United States Government, permission to remain in the State. Many lawsuits followed and continued until the conveyance of title to lands of the Eastern Band as a corporation with the United States in 1925.

LAND

The lands now held in trust by the United States Government for the Eastern Band of Cherokee Indians comprise 56,572.80

which is scattered over five counties and consists of
or boundaries which are contained in 30 completely
bodies of land. All of the land is held in common by
and possessory holdings are issued to individuals.
il of the Eastern Band of Cherokee Indians determines
ement and control of all property, real and personal,
to the Band as a corporation.

ITY

considered a reservation, a land area would have to
owned by the Government and set aside as a reserve
cific use or purpose. Lands of the Eastern Band of
Indians were never owned by the Federal Government, but
hased by the Indians and are held in trust as a corpo-
th the United States Government. Not belonging to the
North Carolina nor to the United States Government,
rn Band of Cherokee Indians exist in the unusual status
reignty within the United States.

e most part, the lands are mountainous with small
long the rivers and streams suitable for farming busi-
recreational sites. The elevation varies from 1,718
ver 5,000 feet.

e last frost dated April 11; average first frost dated
3; average rainfall 47.28" (1950-58); average temperature
s.

N

test official enrollment was conducted in 1974. There
l enrolled members with 5,550 living on Eastern Band
ee Indians lands and 2,831 residing off Eastern Band
ee Indians lands.

T

overnment consists of the Tribal Council and the Execu-
rtment. The Tribal Council has 12 members which
ed for two-year terms, two coming from each of the
townships - Big Cove, Birdtown, Painttown, Wolftown
w Hill and one each from the Cherokee County and
unty tracts. The Tribal Council elects its own officers,

including a chairman, a vice-chairman, both Indian and English clerks, an interpreter, a marshall, a messenger, a janitor and an administrative manager.

The Executive Department consists of a Principal Chief, a Vice Chief, and an Executive Advisor. The Principal Chief and Vice Chief are elected for four-year terms by those Tribal members 18 years of age and over. The Executive Advisor is appointed by the Principal Chief and his appointment is confirmed by the Tribal Council.

In exercising its numerous and complex responsibilities, the Tribal Council relies extensively on the work of committees appointed to work in specified areas. The Tribal Council is basically a legislative body; however, their authority to manage and control the property of the Band, also places them in the position of carrying out judicial functions, especially in relation to land matters.

The Executive Department also functions as an Executive Committee under the direction of the Principal Chief. It is charged with carrying out the rules, regulations, and other actions of the Tribal Council and keeps the Tribal Government functioning on a day-to-day basis.

ADMINISTRATION

In addition to its executive, legislative and judicial functions, the Tribal Government is responsible for the successful operation of the following Tribal operations:

1. OFFICES - Tribal Administrative Office, Enrollment, Maintenance, and The Cherokee One Feather (the official Tribal newspaper).

2. CHEROKEE TRIBAL COMMUNITY SERVICES - CTCS Administrative Office, Police Department, Fire Department and Sanitation Department.

3. TRIBAL ENTERPRISES - Cherokee Tribal Water and Sewer Enterprises, Fish and Game Management Enterprise (includes Mingo Falls Campground), Boundary Tree Motor Court, Boundary Tree Service Station, Boundary Tree Dining Room, Boundary Tree Restaurant and the Qualla Civic Center.

4. PROGRAMS - Tribal Planning and Development Program, EDA Title X, Indian Action Team, Business Development Office, Aid to Tribal Government Program, Comprehensive Employment and Training Act Program, Qualla Indian Boundary Projects--Office of Native American Programs, Head Start Program, Cherokee

Follow Through Program, Tribal Health Coordination
Program, Otitis Media Program, Cherokee Mental
Health and Alcohol Rehabilitation Program, Community Health Representatives Program and the Medical
Aide Training Program.

Operating somewhat independently but still responsive to the Tribe and performing vital services are:

An All Volunteer Rescue Squad
The Qualla Housing Authority
The Cherokee Boys Club:

1. Vocational training and special education
2. Employment and on-the-job training
3. Recreation park
4. Childrens homes (3) and a chapel
5. Contract services (school bus; school lunchroom operation; school and hospital laundry; school, agency and hospital grounds maintenance).

Cherokee Action Committee for Foster Children
Save the Children Federation
Cherokee Activities Center for the Handicapped, Inc.
Qualla Arts and Crafts Mutual, Inc.
Women, Infant and Children Nutrition Program

HEALTH

The major health programs at Cherokee are funded through the Indian Health Service, U. S. Public Health Service. The IHS, USPHS provides regular out-patient clinical services, operates a 26 bed general hospital, contract services for those Cherokees needing surgery and other specialized care and an Environmental Health Office. Many of the Indians still practice the old ways of health care using herbs and formulas either self-administered or with the aid of a "Medicine Man."

EDUCATION

Education has long been the top priority for the Cherokees. After petitioning Congress for seventeen long years, the Cherokees now have a fine new high school which is funded and operated by the Bureau of Indian Affairs. Contributions to our Student Scholarship Fund have made it possible for a few of our Tribal Members to attend college.

BUREAU OF INDIAN AFFAIRS

As trustee, the Bureau of Indian Affairs, U. S. Department of the Interior, maintains an Indian Agency at Cherokee. Its purpose is to help improve the economic and social conditions and to provide guidance in helping the Indians to help themselves. The BIA operates the schools, improves and maintains the roads as funds are available, operates the social welfare and extension programs, manages the timber resources, and generally oversees all matters relating to realty including the records, surveys, leases, business and possessory titles.

INCOME

Direct Tribal income comes from the Cherokee lands through timber stumpage receipts and the lease of Tribal lands. A five percent Tribal sales levy is the only other main source of income.

ECONOMY

The present economy of the Cherokee people is based on the tourist industry which is seasonal, beginning in May and lasting until the end of October. There are over 212 small businesses which are primarily tourist oriented and are 63 percent Indian operated. Two light industries "The Cherokees" and "White Shield" and the service industry "Cherokee Boys Club" provide year-round employment for about 300 Cherokees. A new industry, "Warrior Woodcrafts" is in its early development stages. The Cherokees are a very industrious people. Nearly all occupy much of their time in the works of arts and crafts which are some of the very finest of the American Indian. They make baskets, pottery, beadwork, finger weaving, stone carvings and wood carvings.

CULTURE

Much of the old culture remains, consisting principally of non-material elements. Most, if not all, of the Cherokees speak or understand English, but the Cherokee language is taught in the homes and schools. Sequoyah's syllabary which uses symbols for sounds instead of letters or words has made it possible for this language to be written and taught from text.

Bean dumplings, bean bread, chesnut bread and ramps are a few of the native foods which are still commonly eaten in Cherokee homes. Many still cling to the ancient lore and customs. They sing the old hymns in their own musical language. Some of the older women wear long full dresses and a bright kerchief tied upon their heads. Occasionally, one can see a baby tied on the back of a Cherokee woman.

what is the most popular sport--Indian ball which is similar to Lacrosse, but really a mixture of all athletic games.

Favorite attractions consist of the festivals, the "Old Indian Village," the outdoor drama "Unto These Hills," trout fishing and the newly completed Museum of the Cherokee Indian.

PART 2

REPORT ON ACTIVE JOB APPLICANTS REGISTERED
FOR WORK WITH THE EMPLOYMENT SECURITY OFFICES
AND RESIDING IN THE AREA OF CHEROKEE

I. Recruiting Area

Cherokee's labor recruiting area covers a radius of 25 road miles--approximately 30 to 40 minutes driving time. The area includes portions of Graham, Haywood, Jackson, Macon and Swain Counties and a portion of Tennessee.

II. Population of the Area

According to 1970 Census data, 56,760 persons reside within 25 miles of Cherokee. Of this total, 51,075 persons reside in the North Carolina portion of the defined area. The remaining 5,685 reside in Tennessee.

III. Workers Residing in the Area Available for Jobs

Information compiled by local Employment Security Commission offices serving the defined area shows that there are 2,915 persons who have registered for work within the past 60 days. The tables in the back of this part show some of their characteristics.

IV. Types of Potential Workers in the Area Included in the Report

The report includes only those workers who have filed applications for jobs with ESC offices. Additional workers also can be recruited such as housewives, persons now commuting out of the area, etc.

V. Number of High School Graduates In This Area Which Enter The Labor Force Each Year

For the last school year the number was 200. This figure excludes those graduates who did not seek employment. (June, 1975).

VI. Map 1 (Page 11) - Area In Which Active Job Applicants Reside

The area in which the active job applicants reside is depicted by three centric circles overlaying the map. The inner circle represents approximately a 15 road-mile radius from the selected site. Each succeeding circle represents an additional 5 road-mile radius, E.G.

VII. Active Job Applicants Registered For Work With The Employment Security Commission Office

    This report refers only to the North Carolina portion of the defined area. Additional workers may be recruitable in Tennessee.

Description of Occupational Classes

Professional, Technical and Managerial	Persons concerned with theoretical or practical aspects of art, science, engineering, education, medicine, law, business relations and administrative, managerial and technical work.
Clerical and Sales	Persons concerned with preparing, transcribing, transferring, systematizing and preserving written communications and records, collecting accounts, distributing information, and influencing customers in favor of a commodity or service.
Service	Persons concerned with performing tasks in private households, serving individuals in institutions and in commercial or other establishments, or with protecting the public against crime, fire and accidents.
Farming, Fishing and Forestry	Persons concerned with growing, harvesting, catching, and gathering land and aquatic plant and animal life and products thereof.
Processing	Persons concerned with refining, mixing, compounding, chemically treating, heat treating, or similarly working materials and products.
Machine Trades	Persons concerned with feeding, tending, operating, controlling and setting up machines to cut, bore, mill, abrade, print and work such materials as metal, paper, wood and stone.
Benchwork	Persons concerned with use of handtools and bench machines to fit, carve, mold, paint, sew, assemble, inspect, repair and similarly work small objects and materials.
Structural	Persons concerned with fabricating, erecting, installing, paving, painting, repairing structures such as buildings, bridges, roads, motor vehicles, cables, engines, etc.

Miscellaneous   Persons concerned with transportation services, packaging and warehousing, utilities, amusement, recreation, mining, logging, graphic arts.

Partials   Persons who have registered for work but whose applications have not been assigned an occupation class. Most of these applicants are job ready.

Number of Registered Job Applicants Residing Within the Area

Miles	Persons Registered			With Substantial Work Experience		With Limited or No Work Experience	
	Total	Male	Female	Male	Female	Male	Female
0-15	920	525	395	520	390	5	5
15-20	880	500	380	490	370	10	10
20-25	1,115	615	500	605	485	10	15
Total	2,915	1,640	1,275	1,615	1,245	25	30

Major Occupational Class of Job Applicants

	Total	Professional, Technical and Managerial	Clerical and Sales	Service	Farming Fishing & Forestry	Processing
Male	1,640	185	100	150	60	85
Female	1,275	110	390	390	15	25
Total	2,915	295	490	540	75	110

	Machine Trades	Bench Work	Structural Work	Miscellaneous Occupations	Partials
Male	150	95	490	300	25
Female	100	180	5	15	45
Total	250	275	495	315	70

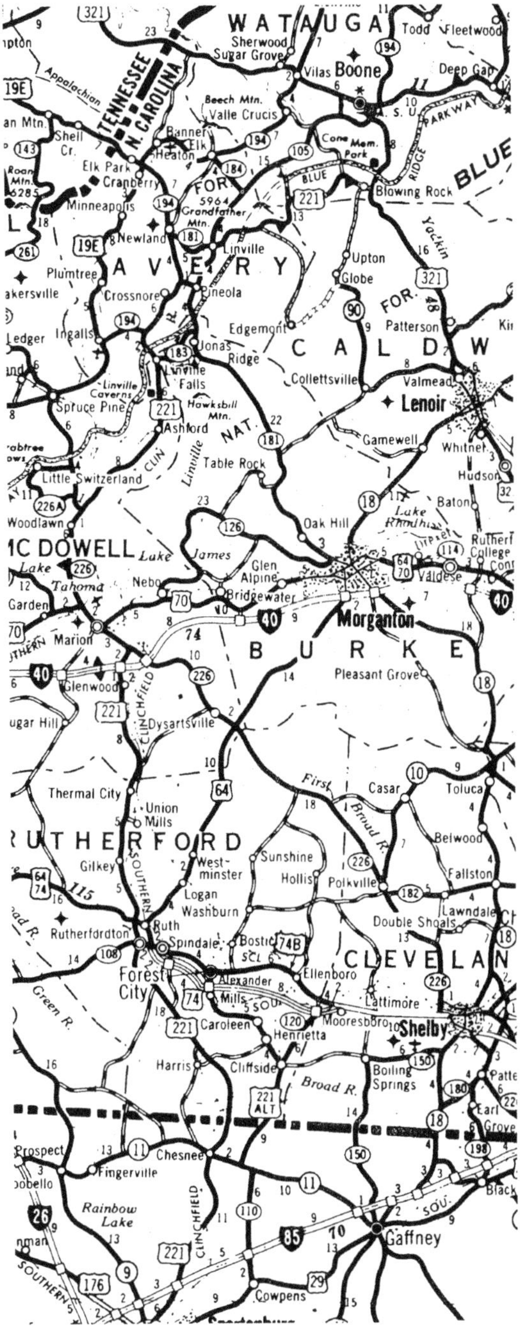
WATAUGA
Todd
Fleetwood
Sherwood
Sugar Grove
Vilas
Boone
Deep Gap
TENNESSEE
N. CAROLINA
Appalachian
Beech Mtn.
Valle Crucis
Banner Elk
Heaton
Shell Cr.
Elk Park
Cranberry
Cone Mem. Park
Blowing Rock
BLUE
RIDGE
PARKWAY
FOR.
5964 Grandfather Mtn.
Minneapolis
Newland
Linville
Upton
Globe
Yadkin
Plumtree
AVERY
Crossnore
Pineola
Patterson
Ingalls
Edgemont
Jonas Ridge
CALDW
Ledger
Linville Falls
Linville Caverns
Spruce Pine
Hawksbill Mtn.
Collettsville
Valmead
Lenoir
Ashford
NAT.
Gamewell
Whitnel
Hudson
Little Switzerland
Table Rock
Woodlawn
Baton
Lake Rhodhiss
Oak Hill
Rutherf College
MC DOWELL
Lake James
Lake Tahoma
Nebo
Glen Alpine
Bridgewater
Valdese
Garden
Marion
Morganton
BURKE
Glenwood
Pleasant Grove
CLINCHFIELD
Dysartsville
Sugar Hill
First Broad R.
Casar
Toluca
Thermal City
Union Mills
RUTHERFORD
Belwood
Gilkey
West-minster
Sunshine
Hollis
Polkville
Fallston
Logan
Washburn
Lawndale
Double Shoals
Rutherfordton
Ruth
Spindale
Bostic
Forest City
Alexander
Mills
Ellenboro
CLEVELAN
Lattimore
Green R.
Caroleen
Henrietta
Mooresboro
Shelby
Harris
Cliffside
Broad R.
Boiling Springs
Earl
Prospect
Chesnee
Fingerville
Rainbow Lake
Gaffney
Cowpens
SOUTHERN

AREA IN WHICH ACTIVE JOB APPLICANTS RESIDE

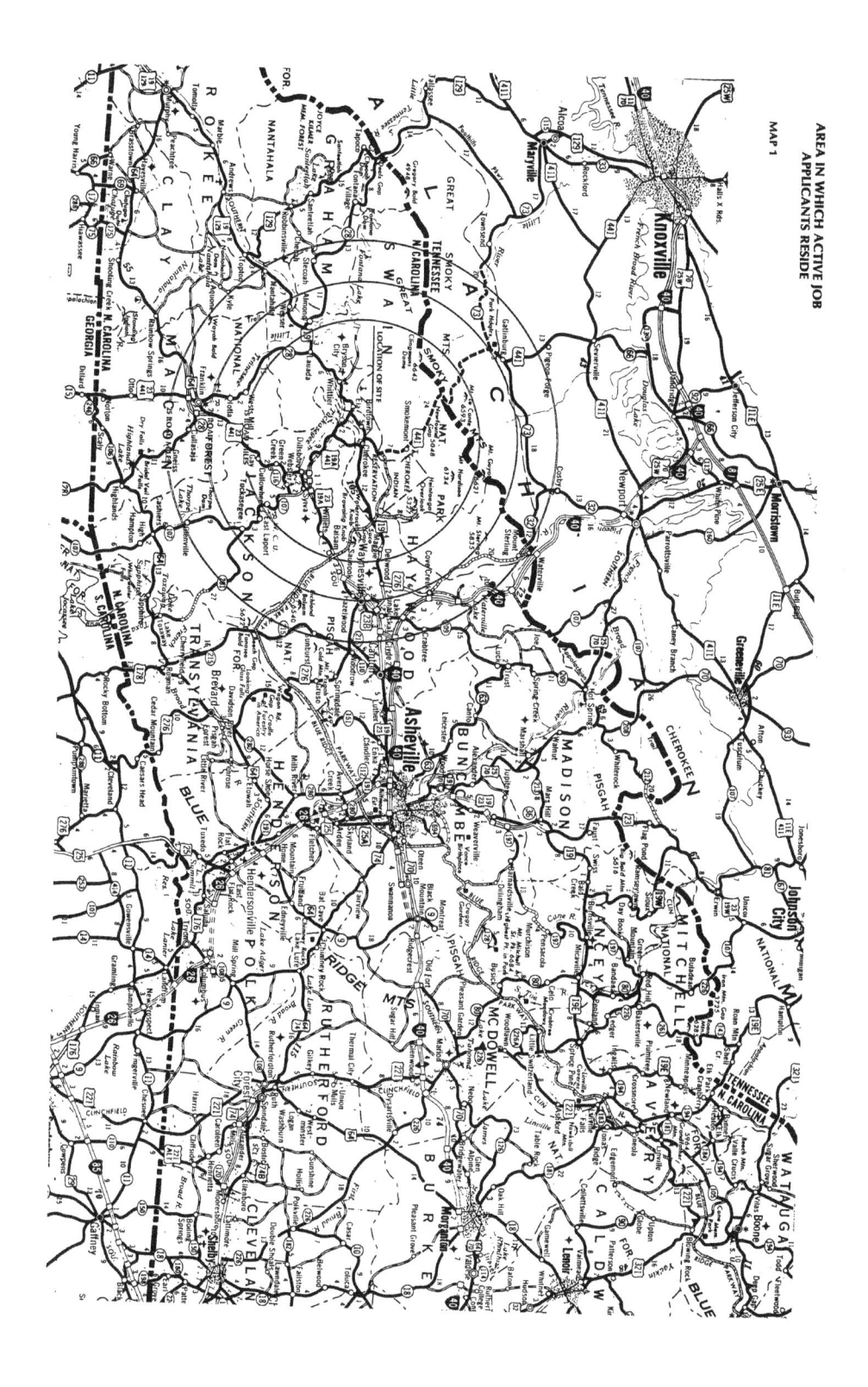

MAP 1

PART 3

INDUSTRIAL DEVELOPMENT FACTS

(EDA INDIAN DESK INDUSTRIAL DEVELOPMENT PROGRAM)

I. Date Form Completed - March 5, 1976

II. Population

Year	Swain County	Includes Indians	Jackson County	Includes Indians	Total
1970	7,861	(2,756)	21,593	(1,963)	29,454
1960	8,387	(2,940)	17,780	(1,616)	26,167
1950	9,921	(3,478)	19,261	(1,751)	29,182

III. Labor Market Analysis

		Indian	Non-Indian
Population 18 through 45:	M	1,035	7,460
	F	1,086	7,180
Male Currently Employed		800	6,700
Female Employed		800	5,000

IV. Beginning Wage Rates - Prevailing Rates

Skilled Occupations - $2.80 to $3.25 per hour
Semi-Skilled - $2.40 to $2.80 per hour
Unskilled - $2.30 to $2.40 per hour

Strikes in the past five years - one strike at Singer.

V. Current Employers (Major Firms)

Name	Products	Employees	Union
Drexel	Furniture	60	No
Skyland Textile	Clothing	402	No
Heritage Quilts	Quilts and Bedspreads	375	No
Sylco	Clothing	425	No
Bryson Manufacturing	Jeans	140	No
National Fabrics	Lace	35	No
Singer Corp.	Furniture	250	Yes
Manes	Wood Products	25	No
White Shield	Quilts	120	No
The Cherokees	Souvenirs	140	No

13

VI. Transportation

    Railroads - Southern Railway
      Number of trips per day - One East and One West
      Reciprocal Switching - Not Available
      Team Track - Available Five Miles From Site
      Contact For Service Information - Boyd Rogers
                                                Bryson City, N.C.
                                                (704) 497-2165

    Motor Freight Carriers - Fredrickson
                           Smith
                           Thurston
                           Blue Ridge
      Number of trips per day - 3 to 4, more if needed
      Contact For Service Information - Wayne Cope
                                                 Bryson City, N.C.
                                                (704) 488-2113

    Highways - Federal: U. S. 441 and 19
               State: N. C. 107
               Other: 4 lane Appalachian Corridor

    Air - Nearest Airport: Ferguson - 5 miles
      Surface: Grass
      Runway Length: 3,000 feet
      Commercial Carriers: United, Piedmont and Delta
                            (Asheville, N.C. - 56 miles)

VII. Utilities

    Electric Power Supplier - Nantahala Power Company
                                Bryson City, N. C.
      Demand Rate: $45.00 first 20 kw
                      1.45/KW to 980
                      1.20/kw over 980
      Energy Charge: 1.30/kw first 20,000 kw
                      .95/kw for next 18,000 kw

    Water Supplier - Cherokee Water and Sewer
      Capacity of Plant: 9.4 million GPD - Raw
                          0.45 million GPS - Filtered
      Consumption: 146,148,315 G-12 months
      Peak Consumption: 78,748,049 G-4 months

    Natural Gas Supplier - None

    Sanitation -
      Method of garbage disposal: Fire garbage and solid
                                      waste pick-up
      Type of Treatment Plant: Trickling Filter 7.3 MGD

PART 4

REGULATIONS AND SCHEDULES
CHEROKEE WATER AND SEWER TRIBAL ENTERPRISE

The Cherokee Water and Sewer Tribal Enterprise of the Eastern Band of Cherokee Indians (hereinafter called the "Tribe"), represented by the Manager of the Cherokee Water and Sewer Tribal Enterprise (hereinafter called the "Water and Sewer Manager"), will furnish water and/or sewage services for eligible users (anyone within the service area outlined on the service area map adopted by the Credit Committee), including private individuals, tribal projects, Bureau of Indian Affairs, and other private and Federal consumers under the following conditions and terms:

I. Rate Schedules: If and when the Water and Sewer Manager determines the feasibility of water and/or sewage services to an applicant, water and/or sewage services will be furnished at the following monthly rates:

   (a) Water & Sewer Rates

       Minimum - First 700 cubic feet $4.00
        700 - 1,400 $.90 per 100 cubic feet
       1,400 - 2,800 $.80 per 100 cubic feet
       2,800 - 13,330 $.50 per 100 cubic feet
       Over   13,330 $.40 per 100 cubic feet

       Water Services Only - 1/2 of the above.

II. Water Connection Schedule

   (a) New Connections: The Water and Sewer Manager will furnish all labor, meters, pipe, etc. for making water connections at the following charges:

       (1) 3/4-inch pipe connections........$125.00
       (2) 1-inch pipe connections.......... 175.00
       (3) 1 1/4-inch pipe connections...... 225.00
       (4) 1 1/2-inch pipe connections...... 300.00
       (5) 2-inch pipe connections.......... 350.00
       (6) Over 2-inch pipe connections.....(According to cost estimates prepared by the Water & Sewer Manager including 20% for overhead).

All pipe, valves, meters, and other parts provided and installed by the Water and Sewer Manager shall remain the property of the Tribe. The water connection fees are non-returnable and shall be paid in advance before connections are made. There shall be only one meter installation per water line connected to the main unless such laterals are the property of the Tribe.

      (b) Reconnections: Where water services have been discontinued or disconnected at the consumer's request or because of the consumers default on payment of monthly charges, water services may be restored at the discretion of the Water and Sewer Manager after the consumer has paid in advance a reconnection fee of $50.00 for each meter to cover cost of labor, supplies, and equipment necessary to reconnect the service, provided the reconnection is made at the original tap on the main. If reconnection is larger than the original connection or at a different location on the main then the rate specified in paragraph 2(a) above for new connections will apply.

      (c) Miscellaneous: Residents eligible for PL-121 projects with the Public Health Service within the water service area shall pay an installation fee of $125.00 for a 5/8-3/4 inch meter, and after the initial installation the published regulations and tribal ordinances shall apply.

III. Sewage Connection Charges: The Water and Sewer Manager will furnish all labor, materials, manhole, etc. for making sewer connections of grade and size, as approved by the Water and Sewer Manager, at the following charges:

      (1) 4-inch service (minimum size)......$150.00
      (2) 6-inch service..................... 200.00
      (3) 8-inch service..................... 300.00

The sewer connection fees are non-returnable and shall be paid in advance before connections are made. All connections to the sewage main will be done under the direction of the Water and Sewer Manager only by a proper tapping procedure. The sewage collection system must not be exposed to ground water and therefore connections must be leak-proof.

IV. Sewer Service Restrictions: The sewage collection system shall not be used for drainage of any type other than disposal of normal domestic wastes. The connection of field drainage systems, even trough drainage systems, and other drainage systems to the sewer mains is strictly prohibited. Usage is restricted to sanitation purposes only.

Discharge of industrial type waste will not be permitted unless it is amenable to adequate treatment by the system's treatment facilities. The customer will be required to provide preliminary treatment prior to discharge to the sewer system.

V. <u>Monthly Statements</u>: Regular monthly statements for water and sewage services rendered each month will be submitted to the consumer between the first and the fifteenth of the following month. Such statements will be due and payable to the Water and Sewer Manager at his office on or before the end of the month in which statement is rendered.

In case payment is not made by the last day of the month in which statement is rendered, the Water and Sewer Manager (effective January 11, 1967) will notify them of the delinquency and if payment is not received by the last day of the month in which notice of delinquency is given he will disconnect or turn off the water supply without further notice.

VI. <u>Use of Water</u>: Water may be used for all purposes but the resale of water to others is strictly prohibited. The Water and Sewer Manager reserves the right at all times to terminate services or restrict the amount of water to be used by each consumer, or stipulate the hours during which water may be used when the sale of water would jeopardize the water service to any school, hospital, or other vital facility.

VII. <u>Continuity and Guarantee of Service</u>: The Water and Sewer Manager will exercise reasonable care in the maintenance and operation of the systems, but does not guarantee that services will be constant. Interruption of services caused by fires, storms, floods, accidents, breakdowns, or other causes shall not render the Tribe liable for damages.

VIII. <u>Service Connection Limitations</u>: The location(s) of water and sewer connections to the water and sewer system will be at the discretion of the Water and Sewer Manager. The water outlet will consist of a connection to the main, water meter and a connecting pipe between the main and the meter. Any easements, rights-of-way, or permits required shall be executed and properly filed prior to any installation. The consumer shall furnish and install all necessary piping connections from the meter to his residence or other establishment. The Sewer outlet will consist of a tap, tee, or manhole in the sewer main with a four to eight-inch diameter outlet. The consumer shall furnish and install all necessary sewer pipe from his residence or establishment

17

to the sewer main. The consumer agrees that all water and sewage service lines installed by him shall be installed in accordance with the Sanitary Code of the State of North Carolina. All installations must be approved by the Water and Sewer Manager.

IX. Maintenance and Repair of Water and Sewage Service Lines: Tribal responsibility for maintenance to mains and lines ends at the outside of the meter and the sewer inlet at the main. The consumer will maintain the water piping from the meter to his house or establishment also, the sewer line to his residence or establishment from the point of connection to the sewer main shall be maintained in good, safe-operating condition at his own expense. The Water and Sewer Manager assumes no responsibility for loss of water or water damages caused by faulty lines or equipment beyond Tribal-owned connection points.

X. Measurement of Water and Sewage: Water used by the consumer will be measured through a water meter which records the amount of water used in cubic feet. The quantity of water measured to a consumer will be used as a measure of the quantity of sewage on which monthly statements will be computed. All meter readings used to compute the service charges for water and sewage will be made monthly by an authorized representative of the Tribe. Meters in service found to be defective will be promptly replaced by the Water and Sewer for quantities of water and sewage based on the amount used the preceding month. Adjustments will be made on the billing the month following that in which repairs are made by taking the average of the quantity metered during the month preceding and the month following that in which repairs or corrections are made.

XI. General: Except for areas beyond the tribally-owned sewer lines, and for temporary construction purposes, no water connections will be made to a private residence or establishment unless a satisfactory sewer connection is made to the Tribally-owned sewer system. The consumer will not permit heavy grease, oil, toxic materials, metal scraps, stones, sand, cloth or other materials to enter the sewage system that would damage or hinder normal operations of the plant.

The locations of meters and connections to tribally-owned mains and lines will be at the discretion of the Water and Sewer Manager. The regulations specified herein shall not be considered to be complete but only the principal guide lines and it is understood that the ordinances and/or resolutions of the Tribal Council now in force affecting water and sewer services or new resolutions implemented or any amendments thereof from time to time shall be binding and all decisions of the Cherokee Water and Sewer Tribal Enterprise shall be final as authorized by the Tribal Council.

PART 5

COMMUNITY DATA

I. Civic Data

    Libraries - 2
        Volumes: 10,000
    Churches - 12
        Protestant: 11
        Catholic: 1
    Medical Personnel - 7
        MD: 4
        DO: 1
        Dentist: 2

II. Accommodations

    Hotels - None
    Motels - 43
        Rooms: 1,009

III. Education Facilities

	Number	Teachers	Enrollment	Grades
Elementary	1	35	752	1-6
Junior High				
High School	1	45	506	7-12
Vocational				
College	1	6	117	

Training funds are identified for start up operations.

IV Public Services

    Fire Protection
        Full-Time Personnel: 5
        Part-Time Volunteers: 15
        Fire losses Last Year: 2
        Fire losses year before: 1

    Planning and Zoning
        Active Planning Board
        Land Development Plan Adopted (See Maps in this
            Section)
        Zoning Ordinance not in force

    Newspapers
        Daily: Asheville Citizen
        Twice Weekly: Waynesville Mountaineer
        Weekly: Cherokee One Feather

21

Radio Stations
   Sylva: WMSJ
   Bryson City: WBNC

Television Stations
   Asheville, N.C.: WLOS
   Spartanburg, S.C.: WSPA
   Greenville, S.C.: WFBC

V. Financial Institutions
   Banks - Northwestern Bank
       First Union National Bank

VI. Taxes
Rate and structure for non-Indian property--$.70 per $100 on equipment and inventory, being revalued and expected to drop to $.40 per hundred according to the Tax Officer of Jackson County.

VII. Resources
Minerals Produced: None

Timber
   Total Acreage: 27,600
   Major Species: Oak and Pine

Agriculture
   Access in Cultivation: 1,500
   Major Crops: Corn, Hay, Tobacco and Gardens

Livestock
   Cattle: Very few
   Hogs: Very few
   Sheep: None
   Dairy: None

LAND DEVEL
BUILT-UP AR

EAST AND
OCONALUFTE

MAP 2

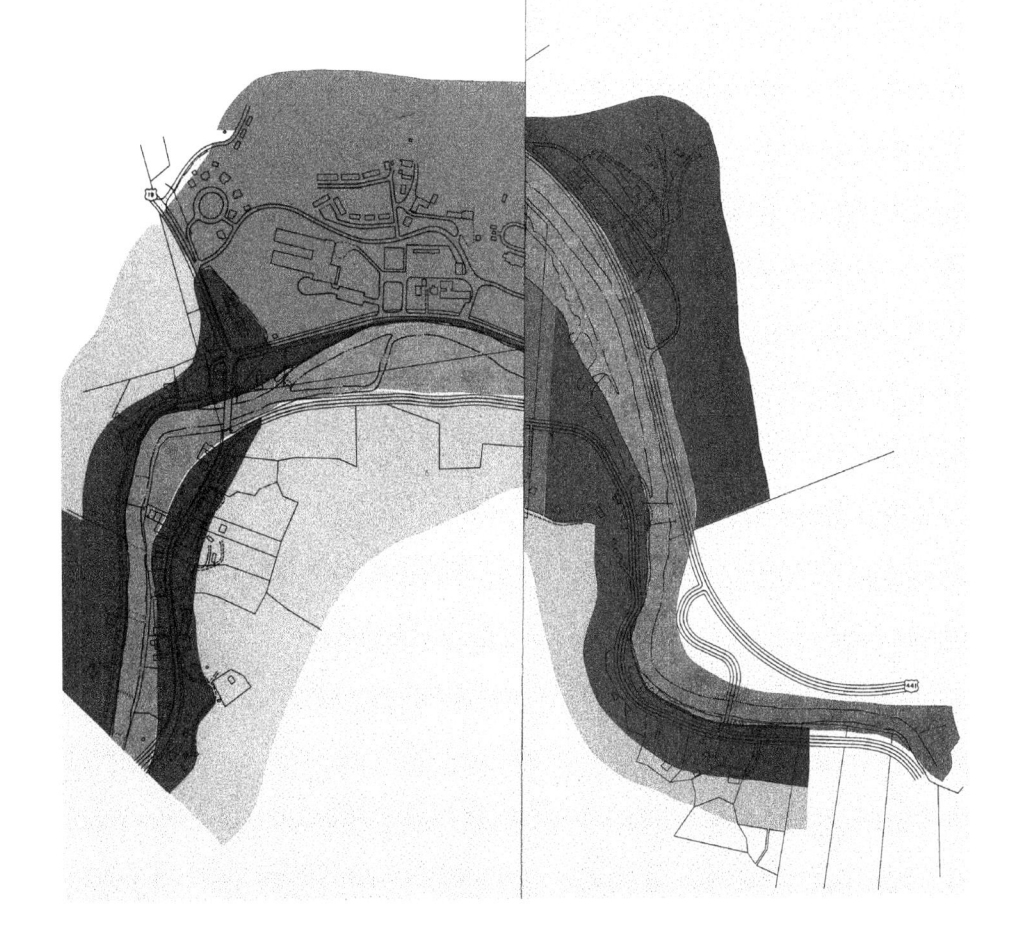

Radio Stations
    Sylva: WMSJ
    Bryson City: WBNC

Television Stations
    Asheville, N.C.: WLOS
    Spartanburg, S.C.: WSPA
    Greenville, S.C.: WFBC

Financial Institutions
    Banks - Northwestern Bank
           First Union National Bank

Taxes
    Rate and structure for non-Indian property--$.70 per $100 on equipment and inventory, being revalued and expected to drop to $.40 per hundred according to the Tax Officer of Jackson County.

Resources
    Minerals Produced: None

    Timber
        Total Acreage: 27,600
        Major Species: Oak and Pine

    Agriculture
        Access in Cultivation: 1,500
        Major Crops: Corn, Hay, Tobacco and Gardens

    Livestock
        Cattle: Very few
        Hogs: Very few
        Sheep: None
        Dairy: None

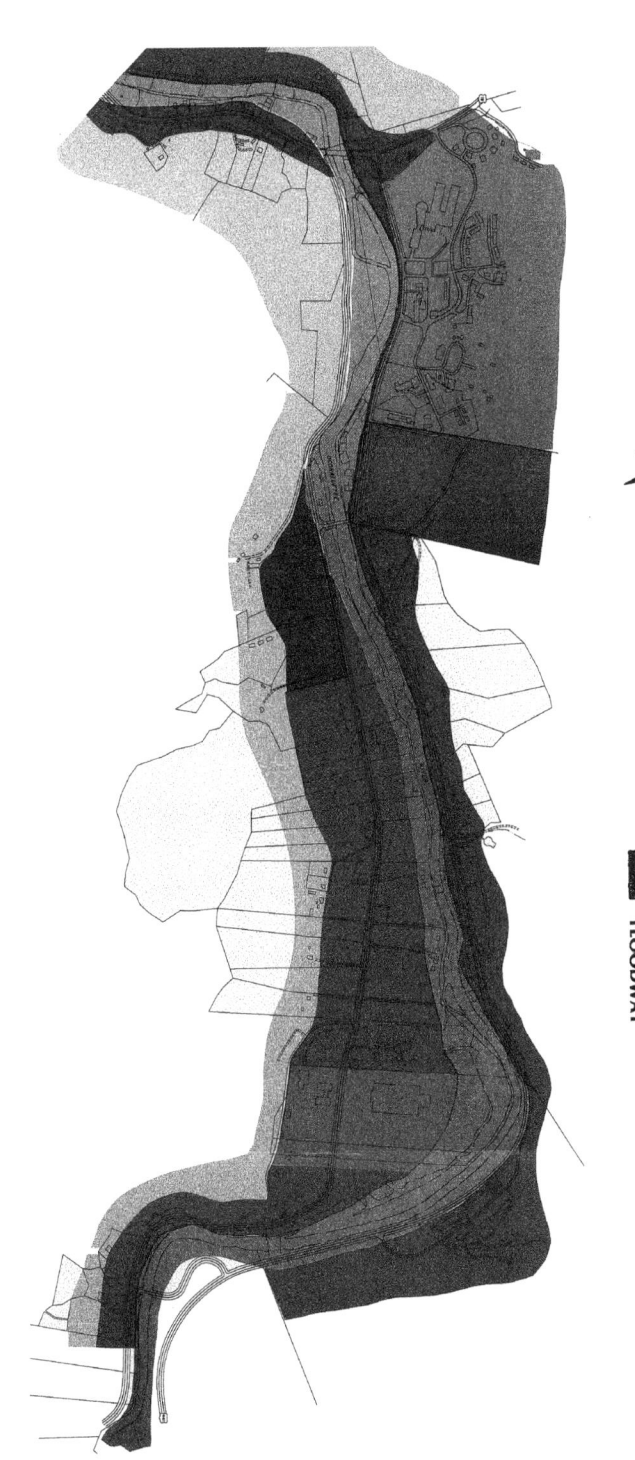

LAND DEVELOPMENT PLAN
BUILT-UP AREAS

EAST AND WEST SIDES OF THE OCONALUFTEE RIVER

MAP 2

LEGEND
- RESIDENTIAL
- COMMERCIAL
- SEMI-PUBLIC
- GOVERNMENTAL
- INDUSTRIAL
- FLOODWAY

LAND DEVELOPMEN
BUILT-UP AREAS

SOCO VALLEY - WEST

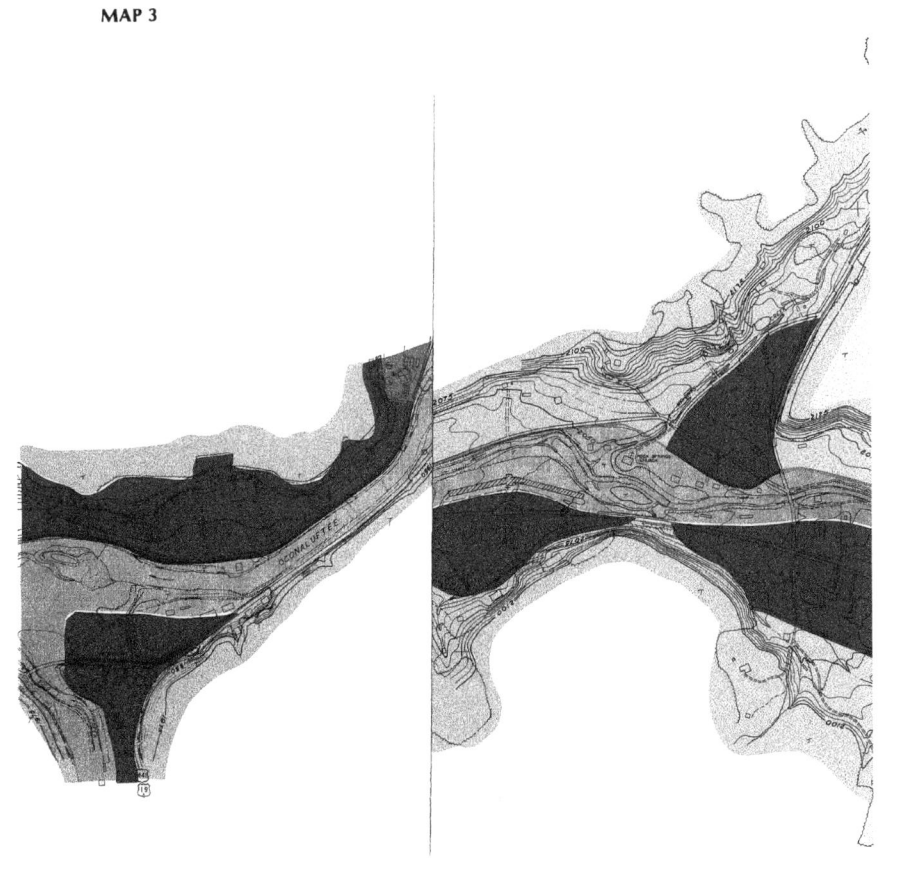

SCALE IN FEET

MAP 3

LAND DEVELOPMENT PLAN
BUILT-UP AREAS

SOCO VALLEY - WEST

LEGEND

- RESIDENTIAL
- COMMERCIAL
- SEMI-PUBLIC
- GOVERNMENTAL
- INDUSTRIAL
- FLOODWAY

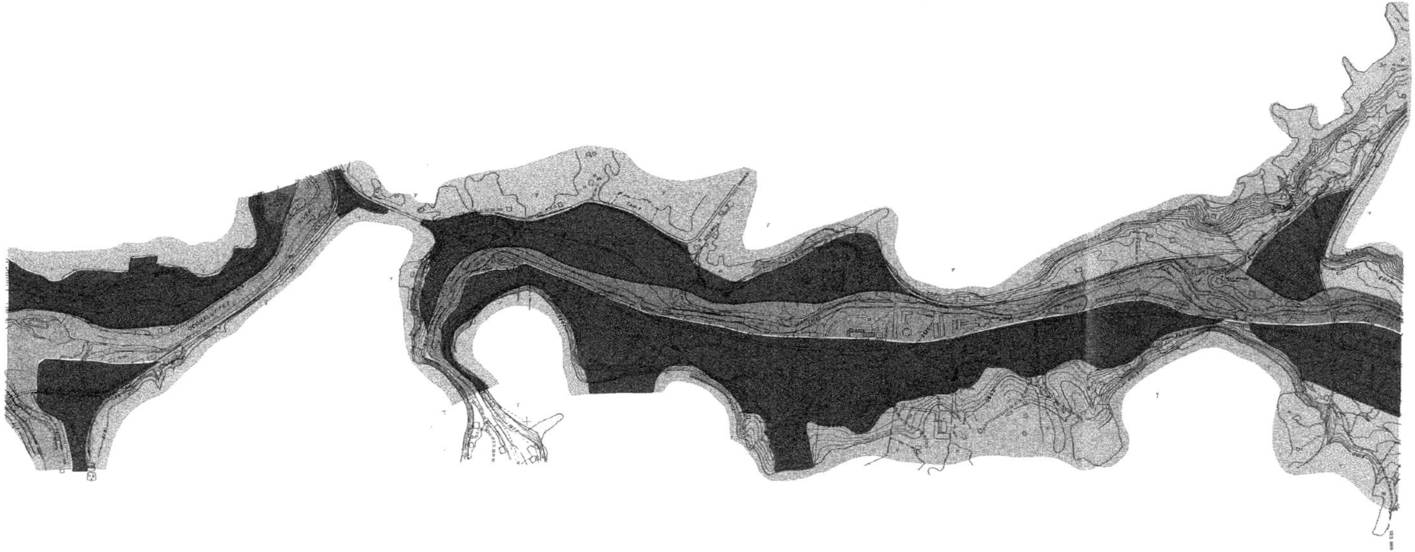

SCALE IN FEET

NORTH

MAP 3

LAND DEVELOPMENT
BUILT-UP AREAS

SOCO VALLEY - EAST

SCALE OF FEET

MAP 4

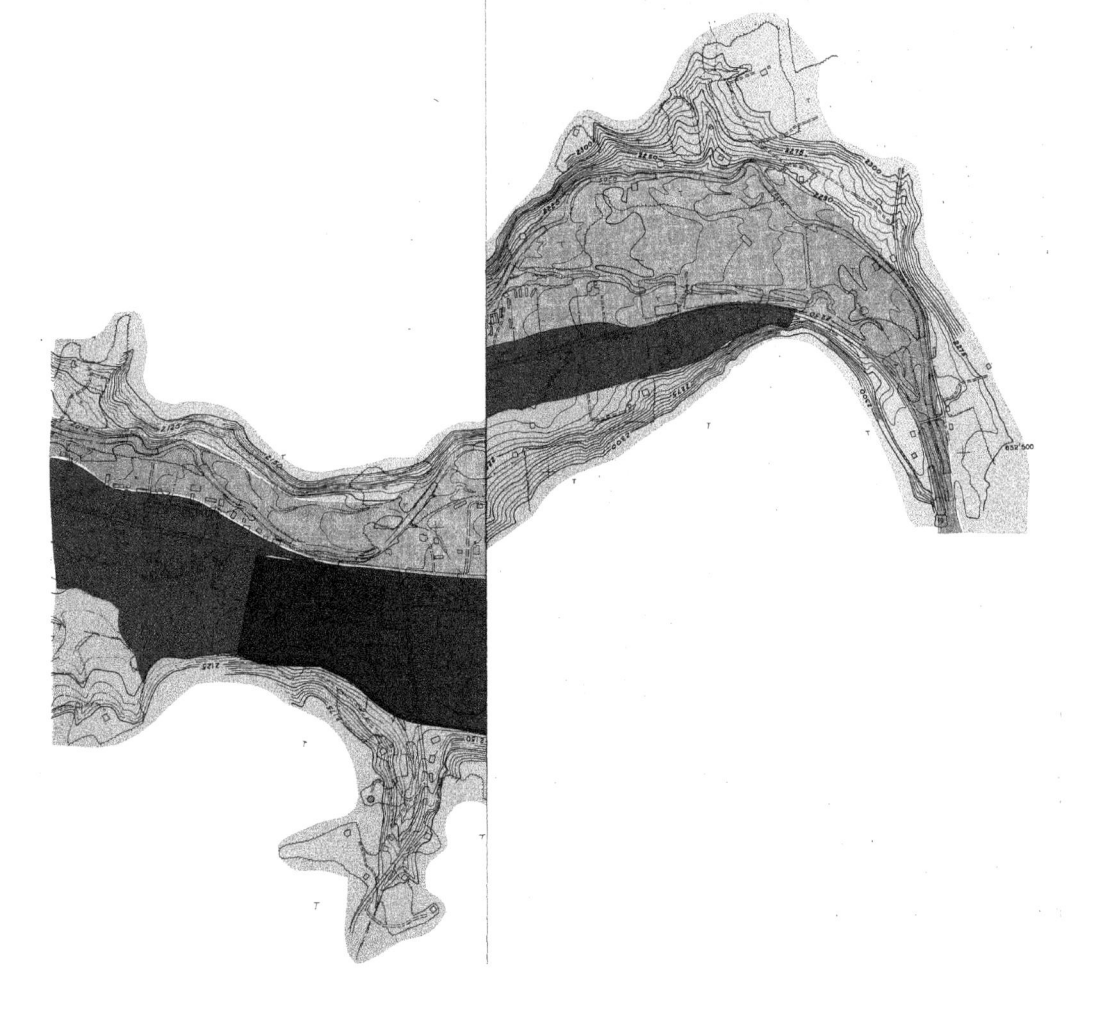

LAND DEVELOPMENT PLAN
BUILT-UP AREAS

SOCO VALLEY - EAST

LEGEND
- RESIDENTIAL
- COMMERCIAL
- SEMI-PUBLIC
- GOVERNMENTAL
- INDUSTRIAL
- FLOODWAY

MAP 4

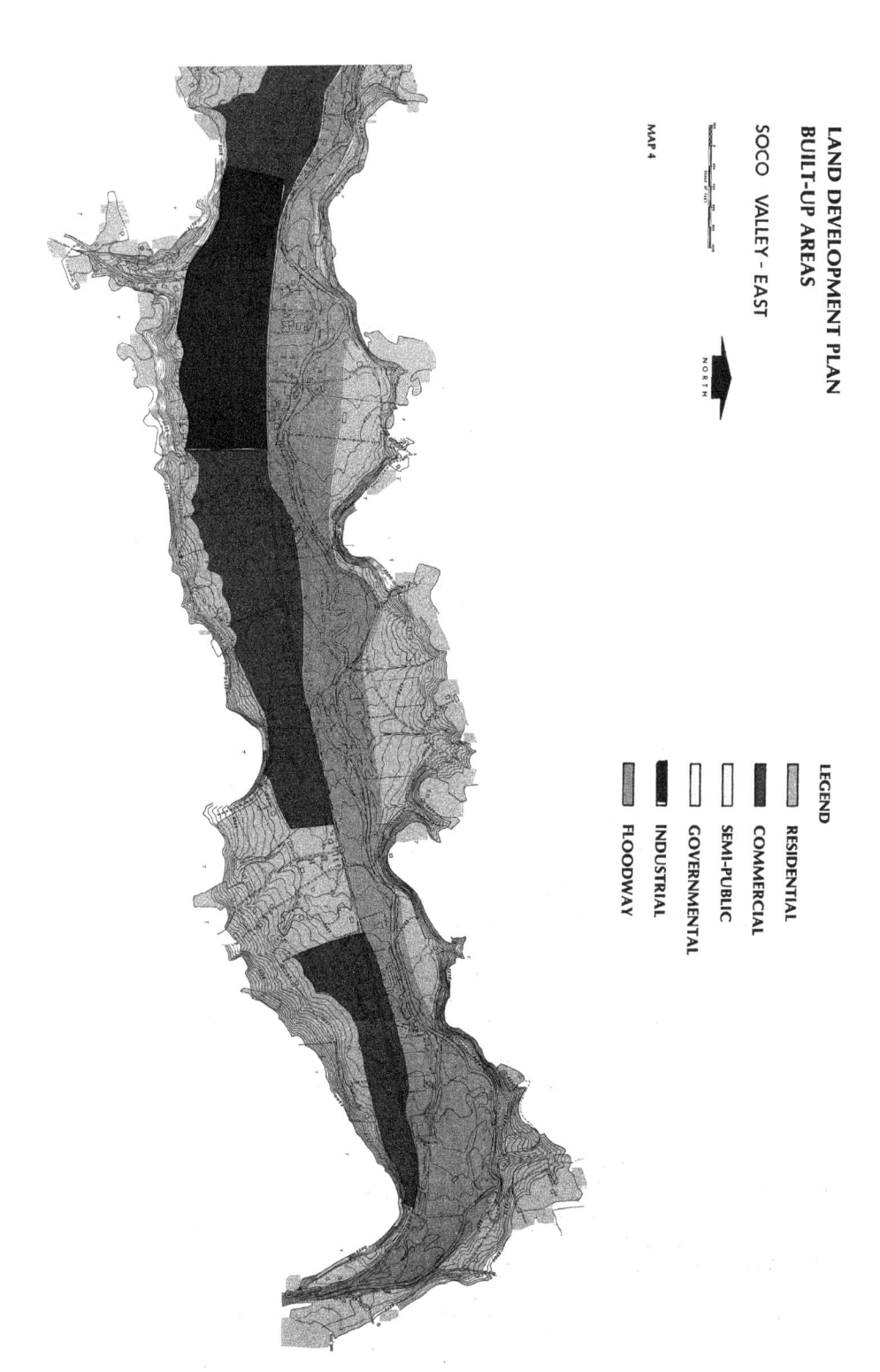

PART 6

LABOR MARKET SURVEY AND ANALYSIS

I. Labor Market Surveys

Three major surveys were conducted in 1976 to provid the labor market statistics used in this section. The Cherokee Planning Board requested and authorized two sur veys to be taken under the direction of the Tribal Plann Bob Blankenship. The surveyors were:

Charles Saunooke - Business Development Director
　　　　　　　　　　Cherokee Business Development Off

Mike Lackey - Business Development Officer
　　　　　　　　Cherokee Business Development Office

Larry Callicutt - Human Resource Specialist
　　　　　　　　　　Tribal Planning and Development St

June Myers - Community Planner
　　　　　　　　N. C. Department of Natural & Economic Resources

One of the surveys was to take place in the last wee of February and the other for the first week in July. T same questions were asked on both the February and July surveys for comparative purposes. It was predetermined the period of lowest employment was the latter part of F ruary and the highest employment rate would be the first week of July. Although the results would not conclusive decide the total number of unemployed in February becaus of not having a means for counting those in the potentia labor force not working or not being able to find work i July. The results would, however, produce a reasonably accurate unemployment rate for the "off season" period. These two surveys included both the Indian and Non-India members of the labor force. The tabulation results are shown on Tables 1, 2, 3 and 4.

The third survey which was more extensive in data cc lected, gives an excellent description of the Indian lat force. It did not include the Non-Indian portion in any of its statistics as the intention and purpose was to de termine the characteristics of the Indian Labor Market c This survey took place in April of 1976 by Robert Evans. Economic Program Manager, Bureau of Indian Affairs, Cherokee Agency at Cherokee, North Carolina. It is higl accurate and exceedingly useful in projecting the number of jobs that need to be created for the Cherokee Indian: See Table Number 5.

TABLE 1

LABOR SURVEY

LAST WEEK OF FEBRUARY, 1976

	Total No. Employed	Male	Female	Indian	Non-Indian
Motel	44	15	29	22	22
Restaurant	30	10	20	19	11
Gift Shop	24	8	16	7	17
Campground	2	1	1	0	2
Grocery	30	18	12	11	19
Gas	20	17	3	11	9
Grocery and Gas Combination	3	2	1	2	1
Industry	277	130	147	227	50
Recreation-Culture	26	19	7	3	23
Construction	7	6	1	0	7
Repair	0	0	0	0	0
Laundromat	3	1	2	2	1
Variety	3	2	1	0	3
Used Cars	3	2	1	0	3
Beauty-Barber	6	2	4	5	1
Bank	6	1	5	1	5
Clothing	5	2	3	0	5
Post Office	6	6	0	6	0
Florist	1	0	1	1	0
Museum	0	0	0	0	0
Sub Total	496	242	254	317	179
Government	890	450	440	711	179
Total	1,386	692	694	1,028	358

TABLE 2

LABOR SURVEY

FIRST WEEK OF JULY, 1976

	Total No. Employed	Male	Female	Indian	Non-Indian
Motel	271	80	191	165	106
Restaurant	408	102	306	218	190
Gift Shop	364	106	258	175	189
Campground	84	56	28	51	33
Grocery	54	32	22	23	31
Gas	59	51	8	32	27
Grocery and Gas Combination	5	4	1	3	2
Industry	263	130	133	223	40
Recreation-Culture	436	211	225	226	210
Construction	5	4	1	4	1
Repair	1	1	0	1	0
Laundromat	5	1	4	3	2
Variety	10	3	7	2	8
Used Cars	1	1	0	0	1
Beauty-Barber	7	2	5	6	1
Bank	10	2	8	1	9
Clothing	5	2	3	0	5
Post Office	6	6	0	6	0
Florist	3	0	3	3	0
Museum	18	5	13	15	3
Sub Total	2,015	799	1,216	1,157	858
Government	1,033	496	537	833	200
Total	3,048	1,295	1,753	1,990	1,058

TABLE 3

LABOR SURVEY

BUSINESSES AND INDUSTRIES   OPEN-CLOSED

FEBRUARY, 1976

	Total No. Surveyed	Open In February	Closed In February
Motel	44	3	41
Restaurant	39	7	32
Gift Shop	70	10	60
Campground	24	0	24
Grocery	19	5	14
Gas	14	9	5
Grocery & Gas Combination	2	1	1
Industry	4	3	1
Recreation-Culture	19	1	18
Construction	2	1	1
Repair	1	0	1
Laundromat	4	2	2
Variety	2	2	0
Used Cars	1	1	0
Beauty-Barber	3	3	0
Bank	3	2	1
Clothing	3	2	1
Post Office	1	0	1
Florist	1	1	1
Museum	2	0	2
Total	258	53	206

TABLE 4

LABOR SURVEY, 1976

EMPLOYED, UNEMPLOYED, PART-TIME AND PAYROLL

	No. Employed In July	No. Employed In February	No. Unemployed In February	No. Part-Time In February	(Underemployed) Total Annual Part-Time	Gross Annual Payroll
Motel	271	44	227	4	231	$ 648,401
Restaurant	408	30	378	3	381	839,581
Gift Shop	364	24	340	1	341	800,630
Campground	84	2	82		82	164,960
Grocery	54	30	24	1	25	132,650
Gas	59	20	39	2	41	208,927
Grocery and Gas						
Combination	5	3	2	1	3	29,000
Industry	263	277	0	1	1	1,595,149
Recreation-Culture	436	26	410		410	950,500
Construction	5	7	0		0	120,000
Repair	1	0	1		1	500
Laundromat	5	3	2		2	18,000
Variety	10	3	7		7	45,000
Used Cars	1	1	0		0	5,500
Beauty-Barber	7	6	1		1	17,500
Bank	10	6	4		4	80,000
Clothing	5	5	0	1	1	25,000
Post Office	6	6	0	1	1	56,000
Florist	3	1	2	1	3	2,250
Museum	18	0	18		18	80,000
Sub Total	2,015	496	1,537	16	1,553	5,814,853
Government	1,033	890	143	15	158	Not Available
Total	3,048	1,386	1,662	31	1,693	

33

TABLE 5

LABOR SURVEY

INDIAN POPULATION ONLY

April, 1976

By the Bureau of Indian Affairs - Cherokee, N. C.

		Total	Male	Female
A.	Total Resident Indian Population	5,633	2,856	2,777
	Total Under 16 years of Age	2,056	1,068	988
B.	Resident Indian Population Of Working Age			
	16 - 24 years	1,053	512	541
	25 - 34 years	834	444	390
	35 - 44 years	569	263	306
	45 - 64 years	788	394	394
	65 years and over	333	175	158
	Total 16 years and over	3,577	1,788	1,789
C.	Not In Labor Force (16 years and over)			
	Students (16 years and over including those away at school	283	146	137
	Men, physically or mentally disabled, retired, institutionalized, etc.	345	345	
	Women for whom no child-care substitutes are available	330		330
	Women, housewives, physically or mentally disabled, institutionalized, etc.	335		335
		1,293	491	802
D.	Potential Labor Force (16 years and over)	2,284	1,297	987
E.	Employed			
	Employed earning $5,000 or more a year (All jobs)	1,008	733	275
	Employed, earning less than $5,000 a year (All jobs)	262	176	86
	Total Employed	1,270	909	361
F.	Not Employed	1,014	388	626
	Of These, Persons Actively Seeking Work	355	150	205

II. Labor Market Analysis

Labor Force - The active labor force for Cherokee consists of 3,048 of which 42.49% are male and 57.51% are female indicating more male oriented jobs need to be created than female oriented. Indians make up 65.29% of the active labor force and the non-Indian portion is 34.71%. The potential Indian labor force is 2,284 and 1,990 were actively employed in July of 1976 which amounts to 294 Indians of the potential labor force were not able to find employment at that time.

Unemployment - The total number employed on the Reservation in July, 1976, was 3,048 compared to 1,386 employed in February of the same year. The percent of unemployed persons was an extremely high 54.53 not including 294 Indians of the potential labor force who were not employed in July. If they were added into the unemployment figures the unemployment rate would be 64.17 percent. This compares to the national adjusted rate of 8.7 or 7.6 seasonally adjusted rate for the same month (February, 1976), a difference of 55.47 percent higher for Cherokee.

Underemployment - Including both the Indian and non-Indian labor force unemployed in February along with the 31 part-time workers at that time, the underemployed or part-time workers amount to 55.45 percent. By adding in those not able to find work at any time (294), the underemployed or part-time workers amount to 55.45 percent. By adding in those not able to find work at any time (294), the underemployment rate climbs to 1,987 persons or 65.19 percent of the total labor force.

Other Significant Characteristics

1. Government employs 29.51 percent of the workers.

2. 34.71 percent of the workers are non-Indian.

3. 42.49 percent are male.

4. 57.51 percent are female.

5. Of the 258 businesses and industries, 206 or 79.46 percent of the total number of establishments close during the winter months leaving 20.54 percent open or in operation in February.

6. Excluding government workers, the average gross annual income per worker is $2,885.78.

7. Those working for industry have an average gross income of $6,065.21.

8. Those working for business alone have an average gross income of $2,408.51.

PART 7

INDUSTRIAL LOCATION FACTORS

Foreword

   The materials contained herein are based on a recent survey of the subject area. This is a compilation of those facts which industrialists are often interested in obtaining. It is not a complete inventory of available economic or community factors.

Community Profile

I. General Information

   Part A. Information for Geographic Entity

      Name - Cherokee
      Type - Indian Reservation
      1960 Population - 33,255
      1970 Population - 39,353
      State Abbreviation - N. C.

   Part B. Growth Community Within Geographic Entity

      Name - Cherokee Area
      1960 Population - 4,036
      1970 Population - 4,881
      1970 Population within 50 miles (estimated) - 387,200
      1970 Population within 100 miles (estimated) - 2,635,800
      Growth Community Is Not A Designated Growth Center

II. Market Information

   Part A. Nearest Market (SMSA With 250,000 or More Population)

      Name - Knoxville
      1970 Population - 400,337
      SMSA Code - 3840
      State Abbreviation - Tenn.
      Road Miles From Growth Community - 70

   Part B. Nearest Small Market (City Other Than Named Above With 50,000 to 250,000 Population)

      Name - Asheville
      1970 Population - 146,056 (SMSA)
      Road Miles From Growth Community - 56

III. Transportation Information

   Part A. Trucking Time to Nearest Market

   Trucking time of morning shipment from Growth Community to nearest market is same day.

   Part B. Other Market Areas Within Overnight Trucking

   Name #1 - Charlotte, N. C.
   1970 Population #1 - 409,370
   Name #2 - Greensboro, N. C.
   1970 Population #2 - 603,895
   Name #3 - Greenville
   1970 Population #3 - 299,502
   Name #4 - Atlanta, Ga.
   1970 Population #4 - 1,390,164
   Name #5 - Augusta, Ga.
   1970 Population #5 - 253,460

   Part C. Highways and Roads

   1. Road miles from growth community to major highway access are 0.

   2. Major highway improvements are underway in geographic entity.

   3. Estimated completion year is 1976.

   4. Paved road is from growth community to major highway access.

   5. Improvements to road leading to major highway are underway in growth community.

   6. Estimated completion year is 1976.

   7. Road miles from growth community to nearest interstate highway interchange are 20.

   8. Road miles from growth community to junction of interstate highways are 56.

   Part D. Trucking and Warehousing

   1. Number of truck lines with scheduled service in geographic entity is 2.

   2. Number of truck terminals in the growth community is 2.

   3. Number of miles to warehouse from growth community is 6.

4. Number of warehouses in the geographic community is 0.

5. Miles to refrigerated warehouse from growth community are 25.

6. Number of refrigerated warehouses in geographic entity is 0.

Part E. Railways In Geographic Entity

1. Number of railroads operating in geographic entity is 1.

2. Reciprocal switching is not available in geographic entity.

3. No rail freight terminal is available in geographic entity.

4. Miles to freight terminal from geographic entity are 10.

5. No team track is available in geographic entity.

6. Miles to team track from geographic entity are 50.

7. No piggy back ramp is available in geographic entity.

8. Miles to piggy back ramp from geographic entity are 50.

9. No freight house is available in geographic entity.

10. Miles to freight house from geographic entity are 10.

11. No rail yard available in geographic entity.

12. Miles to rail yard from geographic entity are 10.

Part F. Railways In Growth Community

1. Number of railroads operating in growth community is 1.

2. Reciprocal switching is not available in growth community.

3. Rail freight terminal is not available in growth community.

DISTANCE TO PRINCIPAL EASTERN CITIES FROM CHEROKEE NORTH CAROLINA

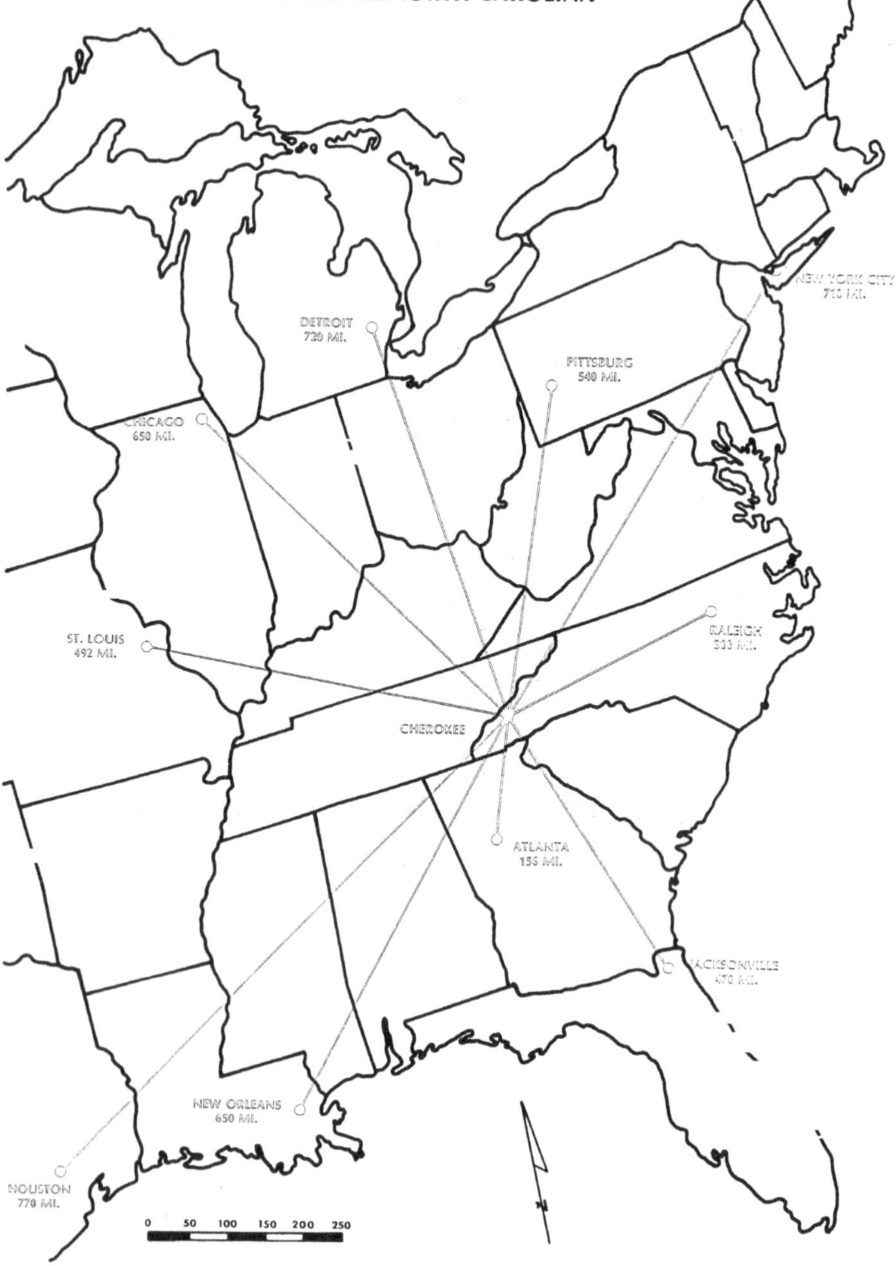

NEW YORK CITY 710 MI.
DETROIT 720 MI.
PITTSBURG 540 MI.
CHICAGO 650 MI.
ST. LOUIS 492 MI.
RALEIGH 303 MI.
CHEROKEE
ATLANTA 156 MI.
JACKSONVILLE 470 MI.
NEW ORLEANS 650 MI.
HOUSTON 770 MI.

0 50 100 150 200 250

MAP 5

4. Team track is not available in growth community.

5. Freight house is not available in growth community.

6. Rail yard is not available in growth community.

Part G. Air Transportation

1. General aviation airfield serving in growth community with a maximum runway length of 3,000.

2. Air freight service is not available to the growth community.

3. Miles to a general airfield with air freight service are 56.

4. Scheduled commercial flights are not available in geographic entity.

5. Miles to a commercial airfield are 56.

Part H. Water Transportation

1. Water transportation is not available in the growth community.

2. There is no potential for a port facility in the growth community.

3. Miles from the growth community to port facilities are 325.

4. Type vessels that are served at nearest port facilities are: Barges
Tankers
Bulk Carriers
General Cargo
Containerized

IV. Industry Characteristics

Part A. Total Number of Employees by Industry for Geographic Entity

Agriculture, Forestry and Fisheries	109
Construction	480
Manufacturing: Durable Goods	570
Non-Durable Goods	1,396
Transportation, Communication and Other Public Utilities	96
Wholesale and Retail Trade	358
Personal Services	576
Professional and Related Services	1,191
Other Industries	814

Part B. **List of Top Five Industries, By Four-Digit SIC Code for Geographic Entity**

1. 2599 (furniture and fixtures) n.e.c.
2. 2392 (house furnishings) n.e.c.
3. 2399 (fabricated textile products) n.e.c.
4. Not Known
5. Not Known

n.e.c.--not elsewhere classified.

Part C. **List of Top Fifteen Industries, By Two-Digit SIC Code for Major Market (SMSA) As Defined in Section II**

1. 50 - Wholesale Trade (durable goods)
2. 33 - Primary Metal Industries
3. 80 - Health Services
4. 53 - General Merchandise Stores
5. 20 - Food and Kindred Products
6. 22 - Textile Mill Products
7. 58 - Eating and Drinking Places
8. 55 - Automotive Dealers and Gasoline Service Stations
9. 54 - Food Stores
10. 59 - Miscellaneous Retail
11. 15 - Building Construction
12. 72 - Personal Services
13. 42 - Motor Freight Transportation and Warehousing
14. 86 - Membership Organizations
15. 73 - Business Services

Part D. **List of Top Five Industries, By Four-Digit SIC Code, For Major Market (SMSA)**

1. 5090 - Miscellaneous Durable Goods
2. 3334 - Primary Aluminum
3. 8060 - Hospitals - Services
4. 5310 - Retail Trade
5. 2011 - Meating Packing Plants

V. **Resource Availability In Commercial Quantity In Geographic Entity and Contiguous Areas**

Part A. **Agricultural Products Produced for Sale**

	Yes	No
Fibers		x
Grains	x	
Vegetables	x	
Field Crops	x	
Fruits	x	
Other Horticulture	x	
Cattle	x	
Hogs	x	
Sheep		x

Part B. Forest Produces

	1st Grade	Allowable Annual Cut (Mil. Bd. Ft.)	2nd Grade	Allowable Annual Cut (Mil. Bd. Ft.)	Pulpwood	Allowable Annual Cut Cords (thou)
Hardwood	yes	1	yes	1	yes	50
Softwood	yes	1	yes	1	yes	30

Other Forest Products - None

Part C. Fishery Resources

	Yes	No
Major Commercial Fish		x
Shell Fish		x
Thrash Fish		x

Part D. Exploited Mineral Resources

	Yes	No
Coal		x
Oil		x
Natural Gas		x
Iron		x
Copper		x
Zinc		x
Clay	x	
Sand	x	
Stone	x	
Gravel	x	

Other Exploited Minerals - Limestone

Part E. Mineral Resources of Commercial Value Surveyed But Undeveloped

	Yes	No
Coal		x
Oil		x
Natural Gas		x
Iron		x
Copper		x
Zinc		x
Clay	x	

	Yes	No
Sand	x	
Stone	x	
Gravel	x	

Other undeveloped Mineral Resources - Limestone

VI. Industrial Parks and Sites Serving Growth Community

Part A. Industrial Parks

	Size In Acres	All Utilities	Air Trans.	Rail Trans.	Water Trans.	Status
Industrial Park #1	15	yes	No	No	No	1

Part B. Plant Sites Outside of Industrial Parks

	Size In Acres	All Utilities (1)	Air Trans.	Rail Trans.	Water Trans.	Status (2)
Plant Site #1	10	Yes	No	No	No	1
Plant Site #2	15	No	No	No	No	1
Plant Site #3	8	No	No	No	No	1
Plant Site #4	5	No	No	No	No	1
Plant Site #5	2	No	No	No	No	1

(1) All Utilities: This term refers to the availability of water, sewer, and sewage systems, commercial power, (gas and/or electricity), and highway access (paved road to industrial park and/or plant site).

(2) Completion Status:
  1. Industrial Park or Plant Site is Available for Occupancy.
  2. Under Construction (to be completed within 1 year).
  3. Planned (construction to begin within 1 year).
  4. Planned (no date set for beginning construction).

VII. Utility Availability in Growth Community

Part A. Municipal Water

1. Excess capacity over peak demand (thousand gallons per day) - 300.
2. Maximum size of main waterline in inches - 10.
3. Lowest rate for industrial use (cents per 1,000 gallons) - 40.

Part B. Raw Water

    1. Well water is available in growth community.
    2. River or lake water is available in growth community.

Part C. Sanitary Sewage System

    1. Maximum size of main sewer line in inches - 10.
    2. Lowest rate for industrial use as a % of water consumption rate if 99%.
    3. Other industrial rate used in $-0 per month.
    4. Sewage treatment plant capacity (million gallons per day) is - 1.
    5. The excess capacity of the sewage plant (million gallons per day) is - 0.50.

Part D. Electric Power

    1. The name of the utility company is - Nantahala Power and Light Company.
    2. The highest primary voltage (volts) is - 12000.
    3. The lowest rate for uninterrupted industrial use (mills/kwh) is - $13.50.
    4. The lowest rate for interrupted industrial use (mills/kwh) is - undetermined or negotiable.

Part E. Gas

    1. The maximum diameter of the main supply is - 0 inches.
    2. The lowest rate for industrial use (cents per therm) is - N/A

Part F. Industrial Fuels

    1. Steam coal is available and the lowest rate for industrial use in dollars per ton is - $10.
    2. Oil is available and the lowest rate for industrial use in cents per gallon is - 15.

VIII. Human Resources In Labor Area

Part A. Labor Force - Current Data (Official Data or Est.)

Total Number in Labor Force	5,590
Number Unemployed	780
Number Underemployed	1,500
Total Number Skilled	Undetermined
Number Skilled - (Male)	Undetermined
Number Skilled - (Female)	Undetermined
Number Skilled Unemployed	Undetermined
Total Number Semi-Skilled	Undetermined

Number Semi-Skilled - (Male)	Undetermined
Number Semi-Skilled - (Female)	Undetermined
Number Semi-Skilled Unemployed	Undetermined
Total Prof. and Tech. In Manufacturing	Undetermined
Prof. and Tech. In Manufacturing (Male)	Undetermined
Prof. and Tech. In Manufacturing (Female)	Undetermined

Part B. Wage Rates (Per Hour Average)

Common Labor	2.00
Light Assembly	2.30
Heavy Assembly	Undetermined
Machinest Class C	Undetermined
Machinest Class A	Undetermined
Set-up Man	Undetermined
Maintenance Helper	2.30
Maintenance Mechanic	Undetermined
Welder ARC/Gas	Undetermined
Inspector Simple	3.00
Inspector Precision	Undetermined
Tool and Die Maker	Undetermined

Part C. Training Facilities and Assistance

	Yes	No
1. Vocational and Technical Education		
Located within commuting distance of growth community	x	
Available to high school students	x	
Available to adults	x	
2. State and Federal Manpower Training Programs		
Any Conducted in geographic entity since 1962	x	
Available in geographic entity last year	x	

Part D. Educational Institutions

	Yes	No
1. Available with Geographic Entity		
Jr. College	x	
4-year college	x	
Grad. Institution	x	

	Yes	No
2. Available within commuting distance of growth community		
Jr. college	x	
4-year grad.	x	
Grad. institution	x	

IX. Community Services and Assistance

Part A. Community Services in Growth Community

1. Size of Police Force is - 20.
2. Community Fire Insurance Rating is - 08.
3. Industrial Building Fire Insurance Rating is - undetermined.

Part B. Assistance to New Industry

	Yes	No
1. Tax incentives available in growth community	x	
2. Tax incentives available in geographic entity	x	
3. Industrial bonds permitted in growth community	x	
4. Industrial bonds permitted in geographic entity		x
5. Industrial bonds approved in growth community in last 5 yrs.	x	
6. Industrial bonds approved in geographic entity in last 5 yrs.		x
7. Lenient industrial zoning ordinance in effect in growth community		x
8. Strict industrial zoning ordinance in effect in growth community	x	

X. Public and Private Local Development Organizations

Part A. Public Supported Planning Commission

Name - Eastern Band of Cherokee Indians
Address - Council House, P.O. Box 455
City, State and Zip - Cherokee, N. C. 28719
Telephone No. - (704) 497-2771
Chief Officer - John A. Crowe
Title - Principal Chief
Year Established - 1967

Part B. Local Development Corporation

    Name - Cherokee Indian Development Corporation
    Address - P. O. Box 455
    City, State and Zip - Cherokee, N. C. 28719
    Telephone No. - (704) 497-4951
    Chief Officer - Lee Craig
    Title - President
    Year Established - 1970

Part C. Local Development Corporation

    Name - Cherokee Land Development Co., Inc.
    Address - P. O. Box 525
    City, State and Zip - Cherokee, N. C. 28719
    Telephone No. - (704) 497-9707
    Chief Officer - Elizabeth Bryson
    Title - President
    Year Established - 1971
      $1,000,000 out in loans

STATE LIBRARY OF NORTH CAROLINA

3 3091 00748 5790

Part B. Local Development Corporation

　　Name - Cherokee Indian Development Corporation
　　Address - P. O. Box 455
　　City, State and Zip - Cherokee, N. C. 28719
　　Telephone No. - (704) 497-4951
　　Chief Officer - Lee Craig
　　Title - President
　　Year Established - 1970

Part C. Local Development Corporation

　　Name - Cherokee Land Development Co., Inc.
　　Address - P. O. Box 525
　　City, State and Zip - Cherokee, N. C. 28719
　　Telephone No. - (704) 497-9707
　　Chief Officer - Elizabeth Bryson
　　Title - President